EVERY SEASON

SHELLEY ROTNER & ANNE LOVE WOODHULL

Photographs by
SHELLEY ROTNER

A NEAL PORTER BOOK
ROARING BROOK PRESS
New York

For Neal, an editor for all seasons
—S.R.

For Jesse, Ian, Julia, Alana and August, with love for each
—A.L.W.

And to caring for our earth so all can enjoy its beauty
—S.R. and A.L.W.

Text copyright © 2007 by Shelley Rotner and Anne Love Woodhull
Photographs copyright © 2007 by Shelley Rotner
A Neal Porter Book
Published by Roaring Brook Press
Roaring Brook Press is a division of Holtzbrinck Publishing Holdings Limited Partnership
175 Fifth Avenue, New York, New York 10010

Distributed in Canada by H. B. Fenn and Company Ltd.

Library of Congress Cataloging-in-Publication Data
Rotner, Shelley.
Every season / by Shelley Rotner & Anne Love Woodhull ; photographs by Shelley Rotner. — 1st ed.
p. cm.
"A Neal Porter book."
ISBN-13: 978-1-59643-136-2   ISBN-10: 1-59643-136-9
1. Seasons—Juvenile literature.   I. Woodhull, Anne Love.   II. Title.
QB637.4R68 2006   508.2—dc22   2006012009

Roaring Brook Press books are available for special promotions and premiums.
For details contact: Director of Special Markets, Holtzbrinck Publishers.

First Edition May 2007
Book design by Jennifer Browne
Printed in China
4 6 8 10 9 7 5 3

I LOVE
SPRING

when grass grows green.

Speckled eggs
fill woven nests.

Showers soak.

Seeds sprout.

Flowers bloom.

Crocuses pop.
Daffodils open,
then
lilacs s p r e a d
their sweet smell.

Salamanders
slither out
from under mossy
rocks.

Ducklings follow,

all in a row.

We hold rabbits,
lambs,
puppies,
and chicks.

Spring
is the time
to dig
and plant.

But then summer comes,
and . . .

I LOVE SUMMER TOO.

The sun
shines strong
and hot.
You can wear
a straw hat, or
go barefoot
in the grass.

Bees sip,
frogs hop,
butterflies
f l u t t e r
and
land.

We taste strawberries, lemonade, watermelon, ice-cream.

Shorebirds scurry and peck.

I hear the
r o a r
of ocean waves.

Summer is the time to splash and swim.

But then autumn comes and . . .

I LOVE
AUTUMN
TOO.

Wind whips,
seeds
s c a t t e r .

We pull up
our hoods
and zip up
our jackets.

Leaves turn

and

fall.

Orange maple, red oak, yellow ash.

We pick pumpkins,

taste apples,

pears,

and pies.

Geese honk
and head south.
Chipmunks
store acorns
in a secret
spot.

Autumn
is the time
to rake
and
jump.

But then winter comes, and . . .

I LOVE
WINTER
TOO.

The cold brings icicles
and snowflakes
that swirl.

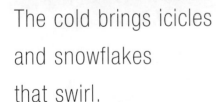

We make snow angels
then sip hot chocolate.
Mmmm . . .

Horses grow thick coats
to keep warm.
Chickadees search
for seeds.

Snow blankets
branches
and buds.

Animals leave their *tracks.*

We wear hats,
mittens,
scarves,
and skates.

and slide.

Winter is the time to coast

But then spring comes, and . . .

I LOVE
SPRING.